This MIT Kids Press book belongs to:

_____

_____

_____

CRUISING ALTITUDE OF TYPICAL JETLINER

34,000 feet (10,000 meters) above sea level

KATHY'S AEROBATIC AIRPLANE

15,000 feet (4,600 meters) above sea level

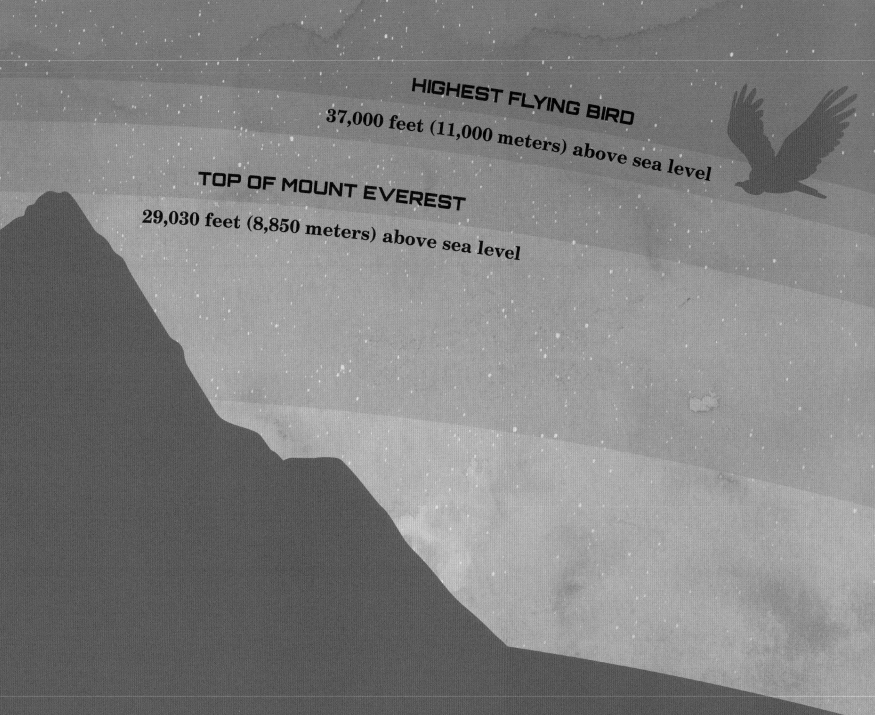

HIGHEST FLYING BIRD
37,000 feet (11,000 meters) above sea level

TOP OF MOUNT EVEREST
29,030 feet (8,850 meters) above sea level

EARTH

HOW TO SPACEWALK

Step-by-Step with Shuttle Astronauts

created by **Kathryn D. Sullivan**, the first American woman to walk in space, *and* **Michael J. Rosen**

illustrated with images from NASA and drawings by Michael J. Rosen

≡ mit Kids Press

So, you'd like to walk in SPACE?

YOU WANT TO . . .

- rocket from Earth in a 4.5-million-pound (2-million-kilogram) spaceship?

- orbit the Earth at speeds reaching 17,500 miles (28,000 kilometers) per hour?

- grab your breakfast floating on the ceiling while watching the sun rise or set every forty-five minutes?

- wriggle into a 280-pound (130-kilogram), twelve-million-dollar space suit?

- gaze across 250 miles (400 kilometers) to the place you call home?

- and touch down on Earth as gently as a jet returning to an airport?

Well, I sure did, but when I was growing up, in the 1950s, girls weren't expected or encouraged to study science. Any science. I have to credit my parents for letting me reach and stretch beyond what might be typical.

I've spent twenty-two days in space on three space shuttle missions. I was the first American woman to embark upon a spacewalk.

I've also charted unknown regions of the ocean floor. I've descended to the deepest trench in the sea. I've piloted hovercraft, hot-air balloons, blimps, small planes, and jets with names like Falcon and Eagle.

Our treehouse?

Nope.

When I was about eight, I challenged myself to design an underwater tree house. Our California palm trees—sky-high and branch-less—weren't really suited for a clubhouse, so my brother and I drew plans for an underwater version on the bottom of our swimming pool.

Little did I know I'd one day be flying in a "clubhouse" that would circle the globe or that my problem-solving and planning skills would be central to astronaut training.

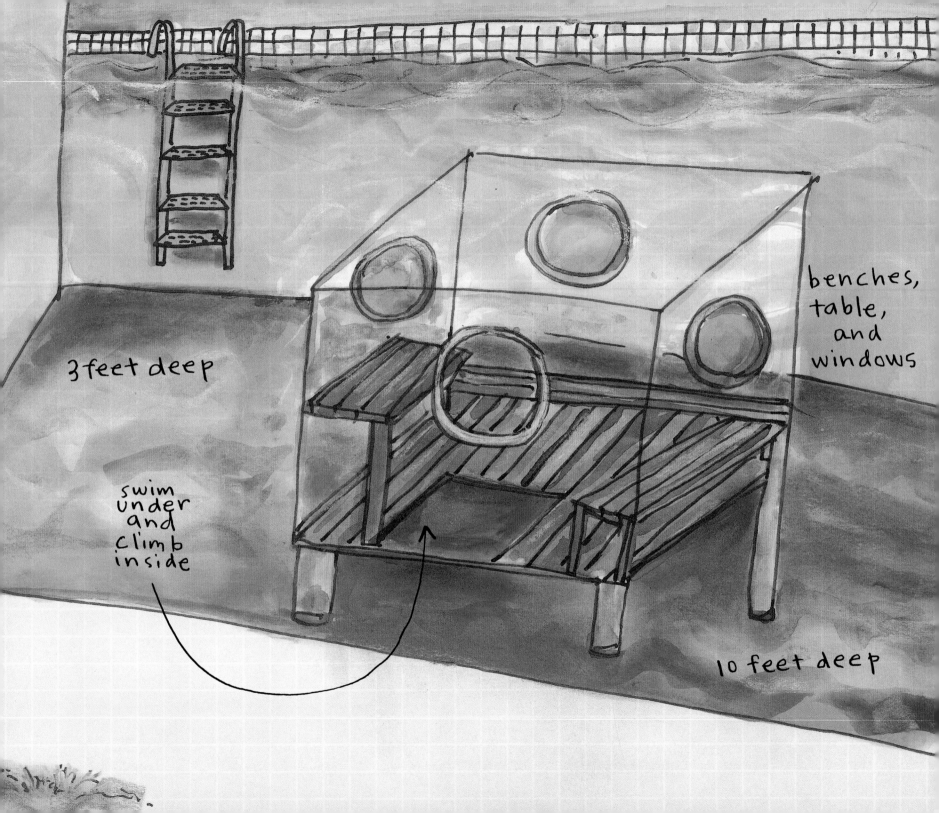

3 feet deep

benches,
table,
and
windows

swim
under
and
climb
inside

10 feet deep

Today the sky's the limit for all kids to study science. So challenge yourself! Let whatever you find fascinating or rewarding stir your imagination and set you on your life's adventures.

Set your heart and mind on something. Work your hardest. You'll be astounded by what you can accomplish.

If you have your sights set on walking in space, you will need a partner. Count me in! I'll walk you through each of the spacewalking steps.

You've already taken the first "giant" step by doing what you're doing now: reading, imagining, and wondering what would happen if . . . Your fascination with how things work, your determination, your joy will all help you find new paths to follow.

WHEN AMERICA'S SPACE PROGRAM reached its third year, in 1961, Alan Shepard became the first American to enter space. Later that same year, I turned ten, and I followed every NASA mission in the magazines and on television. Still, the idea of joining a space crew? I might as well have dreamed of becoming a superhero.

When I was born, in 1951, only two out of ten scientists were women. It wasn't until 1977 that women could even apply to the astronaut program.

My thirst for an adventurous, inquisitive life first led me to study foreign languages. I also trained to be a pilot. I studied geology in college, which offered me travels I'd never dreamed of. I worked as an oceanographer (a rare occupation for women back then). And, eventually, I applied to join NASA's astronaut program.

Along my journey, I readied myself for opportunities and searched for interesting doors that might open new options for me. If they didn't open, I knocked. Sometimes, I knocked harder.

As I was finishing my advanced studies, I was offered two incredible jobs: dive in a miniature submarine to explore uncharted regions of the ocean or join the first class of space shuttle astronauts *and the first ever* open to women and people of color. I phoned my parents to share my news: "I'm either going two hundred miles up," I said, "or six thousand feet down." My mother turned quiet. Finally, she said, "Isn't there anything exciting on the surface?"

THE FEW APPLICANTS that are selected for NASA's astronaut corps have to demonstrate exceptional focus. They need to have earned an advanced degree in a science or in engineering. They have to be fit and in good health. They need grit and steadiness. They must show leadership, foresight, and flexibility. What likely distinguished me was that I had organized and carried out many expeditions at sea.

YOUR TASK: Discover your passion. Fuel it with years of study. Overcome obstacles. Build a strong and healthy body. Choose a scientific field that truly intrigues you. Gather experiences that build your passion and knowledge. And then show what you've got in your application to NASA's space program!

And look! Here you are, acceptance letter in hand, reporting in at Johnson Space Center in Houston, Texas: a freshman space cadet.

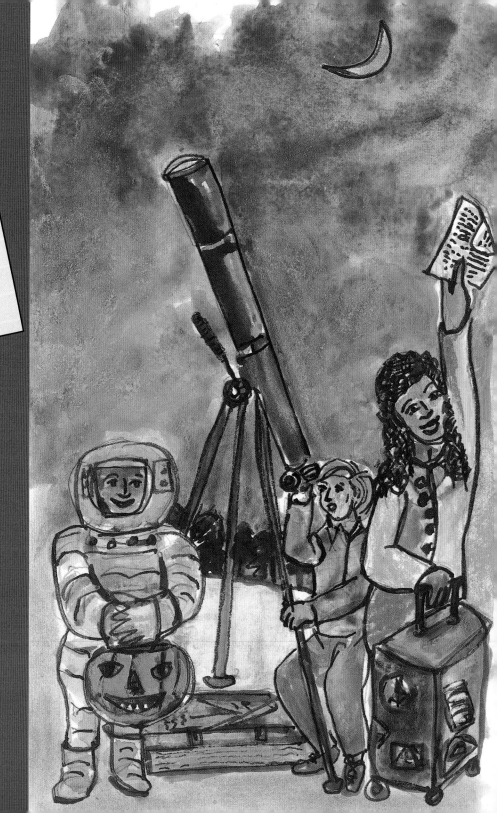

CONGRATULATIONS!

JUST HOW DIFFERENT is working in Earth's gravity from the weightlessness in space? Down here, we'll each need one another's help to put on our space suits. They weigh 280 pounds (130 kilograms)! But in the weightlessness of the orbital flight, everything—including you, me, and our suits—is as light as a soap bubble.

PLACE YOUR HAND INSIDE THE GLOVE.
Yes, that's the actual size an astronaut wears.

LET'S GET YOU TRAINING FOR THAT GREAT SPACEWALK.

Much of our training—I know this is going to sound funny—is learning to be a spaceship. Our Extravehicular Activity (EVA)—that's the official term for spacewalking—will be done in a space suit that provides the same life support and safety systems the shuttle does. Our training drills will teach us how to operate every one of our miniature shuttle's systems. We'll learn how to recharge our suits with water and oxygen, to make repairs, and even to predict possible problems and develop methods to solve them.

We'll practice steering our bulky body-ships and train our hands to work in heavy, humongous gloves.

ON EARTH, our bodies have skin to protect us. That amazing organ can:

- protect us from some of the sun's radiation
- warm or cool us
- protect us from physical harm

BUT IN SPACE, where cold, pressure, and the sun's radiation are much greater forces, we need space suits to:

- shield us from harmful solar radiation
- protect our bodies from frigid extreme temperatures, both hot and cold fluctuations
- prevent our bodies from being hit by even the tiniest object
- protect us from the low, low pressure of space by providing just the right amount of pressure around us

THINK OF YOUR SPACE SUIT AS IF IT WERE ROUGHLY EQUIVALENT TO FIVE THINGS YOU'RE USED TO WEARING:

A SHIRT: The Hard Upper Torso covers your shoulders, chest, belly, and arms.

LONG UNDERWEAR: A Liquid Cooling and Ventilation Garment (LCVG) is a stretchy mesh bodysuit with a net of thin tubes filled with chilled water to keep you cool while you're working.

PANTS: The Lower Torso Assembly covers your legs and feet. (Yep, you're wearing space-booties.)

A HELMET: The helmet locks on top of the Hard Upper Torso and offers you a wide view. You can raise or lower the visor to counter the sun's intensity. It encloses the "ski cap" that houses your communication device.

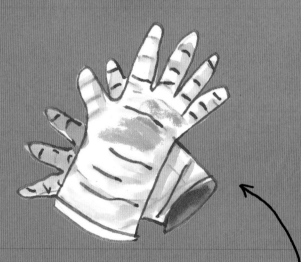

GLOVES: The bulky gloves latch onto the sleeves of the Hard Upper Torso.

Sealed together, this space armor creates an airtight bubble, a safe and breathable environment.

THE ARMS AND LEGS of your EVA suit are a sandwich of several layers. Starting from your skin, we've got:

- a layer of soft, flexible nylon that's comfortable and stretchable
- a balloon layer to hold in oxygen and heat
- netting to preserve the balloon's shape
- a super-tough layer of thin metal to shield you from bits of space junk
- a strong, tear-resistant fabric that reflects heat, light, and radiation

Combined, these layers allow you to withstand extreme temperatures. When we're in sunlight, temperatures can rise to 250°F (120°C). When we're in shade (when the sun is on the opposite side of the Earth from us), temperatures can plummet to –250°F (–160°C).

Our suit of shields also protects us from space dust. "Dust" may not sound dangerous, but anything that moves at speeds such as 17,000 miles (28,000 kilometers) per hour will pack a wallop. A tiny seed can punch with the force of a baseball thrown at 90 miles (145 kilometers) per hour!

YOUR BACKPACK IS YOUR PRIMARY LIFE SUPPORT SYSTEM

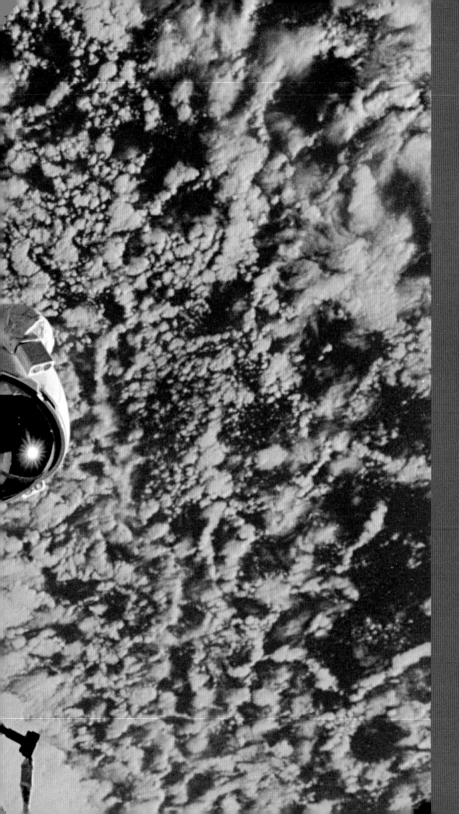

Hitched on to that Hard Upper Torso, your backpack carries in your oxygen supply and filters out the carbon dioxide you exhale. It's also your air-conditioning system: it channels cool water through the fabric that surrounds your skin.

Your body-ship also has room for a thruster pack called SAFER (Simplified Aid for Extravehicular Activity Rescue). If you make a mistake and drift loose from the shuttle, you can use SAFER to jet-propel you back to safety.

Our spacewalk may last six hours or even more. No recess. No naps. And no restroom break: you'll be wearing diapers. (No, I'm not kidding.)

Good thing our helmets have in-suit drink bags. And a food slot with something like a smooshed nutrition bar to eat. Yum!

NEXT UP, we'll practice our space-walking tasks fully dressed in our heavy space suits but underwater. *Plunk!* We're at the bottom of the largest pool in the world. Underwater, we can move in ways that resemble weightlessness in space. We move from place to place, rehearsing using the drills, wrenches, cranes, and other tools for our space tasks.

THIS WILL WOW YOUR FRIENDS: we train in the world's largest pool. A full-size replica of the International Space Station fits inside it.

As weeks pass, we'll smooth out our actions. We'll pick up speed. We'll become so familiar with our "performance" that our muscles will act without our having to think, *Do this, and then do that, and be careful of . . .* Yes, bodies can memorize just as brains can.

On Earth, hands do the carrying and feet do the walking. But in space, hands do both. They get us from here to there, reaching as if we're on a climbing wall, swinging as if we're on a jungle gym. Plus our hands hook our tethers onto the shuttle and operate all the tools.

Try this: Extend your arms in front of your chest and clasp your hands together to make a circle. That enclosure is where all your tools—pliers, wrenches, power drills—are attached.

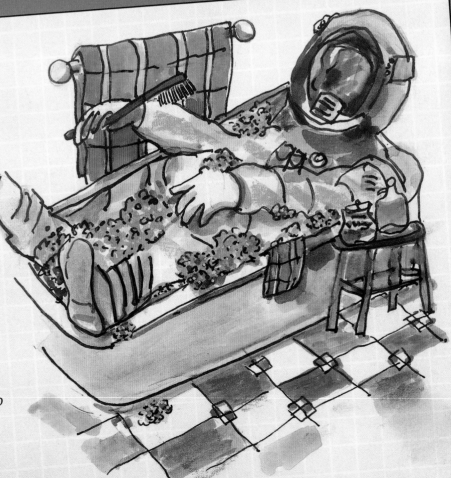

TYPICAL BATHTUB
30 gallons *(114 liters)*
5 feet long x 3½ feet wide x 2 feet deep
1.5 meters long x 1 meter wide x 0.6 meters deep

OLYMPIC SWIMMING POOL
660,000 gallons *(2,500,000 liters)*
164 feet long x 82 feet wide x 6½ feet deep
50 meters long x 25 meters wide x 2 meters deep

NASA'S NEUTRAL BUOYANCY LABORATORY
6,200,000 gallons *(23,500,000 liters)*
202 feet long x 102 feet wide x 40½ feet deep
61.5 meters long x 31 meters wide x 12 meters deep

MOVING IN SPACE

requires a very fit body. Astronauts train to increase strength, endurance, balance, and coordination.

And since our hands take on the brunt of the work on a spacewalk, we do lots of exercises to strengthen our hand muscles, including wrist curls with weights and grip squeezes with thicker and thicker springs.

Before launch day, we'll pack and unpack most of the gadgets and gizmos we need. We'll put them on our space suits and take them off. We'll carry them into a replica of the shuttle and carry them out. Many times. Many, many times. (We won't wear the very heavy Primary Life Support System or the computer pack that controls the fan, pump, communications, and our system's display monitor.)

PRACTICE DOES MAKE PERFECT.

But we also have to practice for the not-perfect: the "Oh, no!" of a communication failure, the "Oops!" of a missing tool, the breaks and leaks and accidents.

WHAT ARE SOME POSSIBLE SPACE SHUTTLE MISSIONS?

- attach a new segment to a space station
- repair, refuel, or replace a part of a satellite
- install a new piece of scientific equipment

These are some of the tasks accomplished on missions during my years at NASA. Maybe you'll be scouting out a site for a lunar landing base. Or even bringing supplies to a colony on the moon!

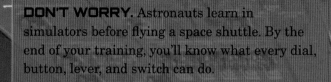

DON'T WORRY. Astronauts learn in simulators before flying a space shuttle. By the end of your training, you'll know what every dial, button, lever, and switch can do.

TIME TO PRACTICE. Yes, again! This time, it's spacewalking *on land*. These "dry runs" are conducted inside an exact replica of the shuttle cabin. Here, we rehearse everything with our IV buddies— our Intravehicular crew members—from stowing our suits and tools to going through the pre-spacewalk checks: check the suit, check the air lock, check the valve that dumps the air lock's air outside—check, check, check! Just like our underwater drills, this practice will help commit our mission's every motion to memory.

Spacewalking is like executing a football play or performing in a dance or band: other people are counting on your timing and performance. (Oh, but there's one big difference: Our space suits' limited oxygen supply won't allow for overtime!)

WHAT SHOULD YOU PACK FOR YOUR TRIP INTO SPACE?

- NASA will supply shorts, pants, and a jacket. You'll want your own undies, T-shirts, or polo shirts. You'll want shoes for working out on a treadmill, but otherwise heavy socks are all you need on your feet inside the cabin.
- You'll want a kit with soap, toothpaste, deodorant, and other personal toiletries.
- On my flight, we packed our own entertainment. But today NASA provides tablets, and crew members can upload books, movies, TV shows, music, magazines—pretty much whatever you request.
- Although there are official cameras on board, you'll want some materials for recording this experience: a journal, a sketchbook, pencils.
- And you can also bring about twenty small items—tokens that will have orbited the Earth with you—which you can keep or give as gifts once you're back home.

We cross the bridge from the launch tower to the ship. Monstrous plumes of what appears to be smoke rise from under its engines. But, no, that's water vapor. Super-cold propellants in the tanks cause the humidity in the air to condense into billowy clouds. The ship creaks and groans as if it were impatient to leap into space.

FINALLY, *finally*, after all our rehearsals, we arrive at the real event. Like Olympic gymnasts, world-class tennis players, singers in the last round of a talent competition—we're pumped, tense, and ready to deliver the best we've trained to do.

Now it's a ride up to the launch pad, and . . . there it is: your spaceship. It gleams like a 184-foot-long (56-meter-long) diamond bullet.

Our ground crew straps us into our seats. They close the hatch behind them. Now it's just us. Everyone else on the ground has moved to safety—miles away—from our launch blast.

We're five astronauts awaiting the signal to blast off.

In our headsets, we hear the launch director announce: "GO for engine start!"

The ship rattles and sways . . . and thirty seconds later:

LIFTOFF!

The rumbles become an earthquake! Our backs flatten against our shaking seats. The shuttle roars as it soars higher and faster, although much of the noise is buffered by the ship's walls.

Two minutes later, the ride smooths out, even as the ship continues to gain speed and height. And then, six minutes later . . . the engines cut off. That pushing-backward feeling stops.

We're weightless. "Hey, grab your pencil before it floats out of reach!" But then, spacewalker, we've got more waiting. A few hours? A day? It depends on the shuttle's overall mission plan. For now, we're IV crew members. We're part of the daily onboard operations team.

YOUR DAY'S SCHEDULE

- eight hours of sleep
- 1½ hours for breakfast, reading, note-taking, getting ready to start your day
- twelve hours of work with one hour for lunch
- one hour for exercise (buckling into a stationary bike or treadmill)
- 1½ hours for dinner, writing, reading, and winding down to sleep

LIVING QUARTERS
OF THE SHUTTLE

- The upper deck houses our flight controls and communication systems.
- The mid-deck is our storage and living space. We'll sleep, eat, read, wash up, and exercise here, and sometimes do some scientific work. The air lock and our space suits are also located here.
- The lower deck is the shuttle's mechanical room, housing pumps, fans, motors, water tanks, and garbage bins.

body wash

squeeze packet of water

AT LAST, it's our EVA day. The day we've rehearsed for months. We float toward the air lock. (Stay calm. We've got this, partner.) An IV buddy comes along to help us get into our suits and do all the safety checks.

FIRST, squiggle into your LCVG, the "long underwear" with the cooling tubes.

RUB a tiny bit of dish soap on the inside of your helmet so your breath won't fog the visor.

NEXT, pull on your Lower Torso Assembly.

NOW it's into the air lock, where the Upper Torso and helmet are charged and ready. Here's where we definitely need our IV buddy's help.

SQUIRM into your Upper Torso.

BE PATIENT as your IV buddy slides on the hood that holds your microphone.

YANK on those giant gloves and lock them to your sleeves.

SETTLE your helmet into place and lock it down.

EARTH'S AIR—and every breath we take in—is 78 percent nitrogen, a gas our bodies don't use. To get our bodies ready for the lower pressure and all-oxygen environment inside our space suits, we have to release that nitrogen—over time. Think of yourself as a bottle of warm soda. You want to untwist the cap slowly and release the gas inside gently . . . in little bubbles instead of a fizzy explosion. So we take those forty minutes to let the nitrogen seep out of our bodies.

nice and slow

TOO FAST!

HERE WE ARE, sealed in our suits, two ready "spaceships" in the mother ship that brought us. For the next forty minutes, we stay in the air lock and breathe the pure oxygen inside our suits to get our bodies ready for when all the air is dumped out of the air lock and we head outside.

When we're done, and when Mission Control gives us the go, I open a valve on the outer hatch to let the air in the lock escape into space. When there is no air pressure inside and out, it's time for those words you've anticipated ever since you joined the space program . . .

• • •

Are you thinking, *Will I suddenly be scared? Will I want to turn back?*

TRUST ME: You won't. Your doubts and fears? You left them back on Earth. Right now, your study, practice, and training have kicked in. You'll be calm. Focused. Raring to go! And I'm right beside you, partner.

"YOU ARE GO FOR EVA."

It's Mission Control broadcasting in our helmets.

Open the outer hatch. Connect your tether to the safety wire on the ship's hull. And . . . here we go, floating into space! Mission about-to-be-accomplished!

LET'S GET SPACEWALKING!

← That's me on the right.

As our feet float free, we're like ninjas, swinging, grabbing, and climbing across the shuttle. We have no more weight than a blink or a smile.

Now, with your feet locked in place, your hands ready for their first task, take a moment, my friend, to realize just where you are and how you got here! You started with a sky-high wish, a drive to fulfill a lofty dream, and today, all your years of dedicated work have "landed" you right here. Yep, 250 miles (400 kilometers) above that big blue-and-green planet!

ON EARTH, gravity makes actions like closing a door or turning a knob easy. But while we're weightless, we can't apply any force unless we're anchored. If you tried to tighten a bolt without first locking your feet in place, you and the wrench would just revolve around the bolt!

LISTEN UP!

Sounds don't travel in the vacuum of space. But you can hear me through your radio, and you can hear the vibrations of the fans and motors of your suit. What's more, our fellow crew members and the folks at Mission Control are monitoring our progress and coaching us along the way.

That's me on my first shuttle mission.

"Heads up! Seven minutes to sunset: adjust your helmet lights."

"We're running behind. Prep for the next task."

"Hey, partner, I bet you never imagined it would be this much fun!"

"Check out those shooting stars under us! This has got to be the best, seeing them from above!"

A METEOR IS A SPACE ROCK,

a chunk of an asteroid (a much larger space rock). On Earth, we spot them as fiery streaks as they enter our skies, about 35 miles (56 kilometers) above us. Friction in our atmosphere is what causes them to burn. Rub your hand back and forth across the carpet; your skin gets hot. That's friction. If the sky were a carpet and a meteor were your hand, hurtling faster and faster toward Earth, you can see how that "rubbing" would cause the rock to burn up.

LOOK AT THAT!

Remember: your helmet can't rotate—it's part of your airtight shell. If you want to look left or right, swivel your entire body in that direction.

TAKE YOUR TIME!

You can't fall in space, but you can drift off. So, like a mountain climber, always keep yourself tethered as you move. Hook on a new tether before you unhook the last one. Lock a boot in place: *click*. Secure a hand grip: check!

HOLD TIGHT!

Even though your gloves with their metal and fiber supports were custom-fit to your hands, every grip requires real force. Hooking and unhooking safety tethers, grasping power drills and robot cranes, and clutching hand-rails (hundreds of times during our EVA)—all that exhausts the hand and forearm muscles.

HANG ON!

Just as you always link to the spacecraft, your tools always link to you. They float on their tethers like thought bubbles in a cartoon of you. Your hand's every shift sets the tools in motion.

ON A SPACEWALK, you must never look at the sun. On Earth, it can be painful and harmful to look at the bright sun; on a spacewalk, the light is even more intense without the filter of the Earth's atmosphere. Here's a tip, partner: turn your back to the sun, and you can see how it illuminates our home planet.

So glad to have your help.
We pull ourselves back into the
air lock and shut the outer hatch.
Now our helmets fill with the cheers
of congratulations!

GREAT WORK!

Once both sides of the cabin door have equal pressure, our IV buddy opens the hatch and comes in to help us out of our suits. We pop off our helmets—ah, the rush of fresh air!—squirm out of the Upper Torso, and float back into the cabin. We did it!

We've just accomplished something that so many people have dreamed about but only the fewest have experienced.

After such extraordinary efforts, we are ready for an ordinary, home-cooked meal—I mean, space dinner.

How could anything prepare you for seeing the Earth without even the frame of a window?

Or seeing the very shuttle you blasted off in from the outside?

Nothing could prepare you for that thrill of weightlessness—AM I RIGHT?

It has to be the most GIDDY, UNBELIEVABLE EXPERIENCE EVER.

LIKEWISE, all those photos or videos you've seen of Earth can't equal the magnificence of seeing it float like a blue beach ball spinning in the dark of space.

Mission Control continues to send us cheers and congratulations as we prepare for the ride home: forms, charts, and logs have to be completed. We're IV crew members again.

Buckled in for our descent, relief and pride fill the cabin just like breathable air. Everyone's joking around. Someone says, "Let's bet on when the dirty laundry bag, floating at the end of its rope, drops to the deck."

The engines slow the shuttle by about 200 miles (320 kilometers) per hour, just enough to let gravity bend our flight path down toward Earth. Get ready for the second ride of your life: forty minutes when we're in free fall, just like a skydiver before the parachute is pulled. When we reach Earth's atmosphere, the spaceship slows down. Our seat belts force us backward in our seats. Gravity presses against our bodies again; our arms feel oddly heavy. The shuttle slows and slows . . .

Unlike earlier spacecraft, we don't have to plunk into the ocean to be retrieved by a ship. We can glide onto a runway.

Unbuckle your harness, but don't rush to stand. Your suddenly heavy body needs to readjust to gravity. As you wait—a little wobbly—for the engineers to open the hatch, you might be thinking: *How could our mission be so surprising and amazing when we've had months of rehearsals and simulations?*

First, we still felt gravity in the underwater sessions. Up was up. Down was down. But in orbit, "up" and "down" were wherever we chose: wall, floor, and ceiling. That's some crazy fun.

And, second, buoyancy in water can't compare to floating in space. We have now just swung around on the solar system's coolest jungle gym. And Earth was right above us—or below us.

It will take many days, or even months, to fully appreciate what you've just experienced. You, partner, now have a unique place in space-flight and science history. The steps you took in preparation for, and during, your spacewalk will shadow you—will *lead* you—the rest of the life you invent.

49

A NOTE FROM MICHAEL J. ROSEN

I met Kathy Sullivan in Columbus, Ohio, after she completed a decade directing the local science museum. She was seeking a writing partner. I was thrilled to consider a project with a three-time shuttle astronaut, explorer, ocean-ographer—a woman whose contagious, coura-geous passion and unique insights deserve the widest audience.

We started meeting regularly to try out ideas. One such meeting took place at a small airfield where Kathy housed *Miss Scarlett*, her two-seater airplane. She strapped me into the back seat, secured my headphones, and lifted us above the county for a few circles. Had I ever flown with an astronaut? Had I ever flown in a tiny plane? Had I ever experienced the real pull of Earth's gravity as she nose-dived toward the ground? No, no, and *OH no*.

My amazement at Kathy's accomplishments on land, under the sea, and in the sky led me to call her "the most vertical person in the world." (In 2020, she added miles to that span by descending to the deepest part of the ocean in a submersible. She now holds three Guinness world records for her accomplishments.) I feel such joy in being able to bring some of her first-hand knowledge and dazzling accom-plishments to young readers.

Kathy, the pilot, with 3,000 hours in the air.
Michael, the passenger, with 596,020 hours on the ground.

INVESTIGATE!
HOW TO SPACEWALK

- Spacewalking is like executing a football play or a dance routine. Get a group of your friends together and come up with a series of movements that you think astronauts would perform in space. Rehearse it enough so that your muscles learn how to do it without thinking. Put on a show for your friends and family!

- Astronauts can take twenty small items into orbit with them that they can give out as gifts when they return. Make a list of ten things you would bring and write why each one is on your list.

- A day has twenty-four hours in it. Astronauts have a pre-scribed schedule for everything they do in that time. Create a schedule of your day that adds up to twenty-four hours.

- What do you think would be the most fun part of being an astronaut and walking in space? Write a short story about it!

Text copyright © 2023 by Kathryn D. Sullivan
and Michael J. Rosen
Illustrations copyright © 2023 by Michael J. Rosen

All photographs are courtesy of the National
Aeronautics and Space Administration (NASA) except
those on pages 4–5, which are courtesy of Kathryn D. Sullivan.

The MIT Press, the ≡mit Kids Press colophon, and MIT Kids Press are trademarks
of The MIT Press, a department of the Massachusetts Institute of Technology,
and used under license from The MIT Press. The colophon and MIT Kids Press
are registered in the US Patent and Trademark Office.

First paperback edition 2024

Library of Congress Catalog Card Number 2022907009
ISBN 978-1-5362-2621-8 (hardcover)
ISBN 978-1-5362-3270-7 (paperback)

LEO 29 28 27 26 25 24
10 9 8 7 6 5 4 3 2 1

Printed in Heshan, Guangdong, China

This book was typeset in New Century Schoolbook.
The illustrations were done in ink and pastel.

MIT Kids Press
an imprint of Candlewick Press
99 Dover Street
Somerville, Massachusetts 02144

mitkidspress.com
candlewick.com

ORBIT OF THE MOON

↑ 225,623–252,088 miles (363,000–406,000 kilometers) above Earth

ORBIT OF THE INTERNATIONAL SPACE STATION

240 miles (390 kilometers) above Earth

ORBIT OF THE HUBBLE SPACE TELESCOPE
340 miles (547 kilometers) above Earth

ORBIT OF THE SPACE SHUTTLE
190–330 miles (306–530 kilometers) above Earth

EARTH

KATHRYN D. SULLIVAN, dubbed "the most vertical woman in the world" by coauthor Michael J. Rosen, has spanned the greatest vertical distance that any earthling has traveled, from the deepest ocean to the altitudes of three space shuttle missions. Among the first women in the US space program and the first American woman to conduct a spacewalk, she is also an oceanographer, global explorer, and pilot, as well as the author of *Handprints on Hubble*. For several years, she served as an under secretary of the National Oceanic and Atmospheric Administration (NOAA). She lives in Ohio with a pair of Havanese pooches.

MICHAEL J. ROSEN is the author of some 150 books for readers of all ages, including *A Ben of All Trades: The Most Inventive Boyhood of Benjamin Franklin*, *The Tale of Rescue*, and four volumes of haiku. His imagination has soared in many directions and genres over forty years of writing, yet the one he's never considered is *up*: a step stool is his maximum height, and a sheet of black construction paper on the floor makes him dizzy. He lives in the Appalachian foot-hills of Ohio, where he also works as a painter, sculptor, and print-maker and as the companion animal to a cattle dog named Chant.